I0767673

ADHD IN CHILDREN
CAUSES, ADVICE AND THERAPY
MY ADHD MIND
LENA LUDWIG

Introduction to ADHD in children

ADHD (attention-deficit/hyperactivity disorder) is a neurological disorder that manifests in childhood and is characterized by a pattern of symptoms that cause problems with attention, impulse control, and hyperactivity. Symptoms of ADHD in children include: Inattention: children with ADHD have difficulty focusing on one thing and completing tasks. They can be easily distracted, are forgetful and cannot follow instructions well. Hyperactivity: Children with ADHD are often restless, fidgety and have difficulty sitting still or staying quiet. They often cannot wait for their turn and may burst into conversations or activities. Impulsivity: Children with ADHD often act impulsively and without thinking. They may have difficulty controlling their impulses, which can lead to mistakes and accidents. The causes of ADHD are not fully understood, but both genetic and environmental factors are thought to play a role. Treatment for ADHD in children often involves a combination of medication and behavioral interventions such as therapy, parent training and school support. It is important to note that not all children who have difficulty concentrating or sitting still have ADHD. If parents or teachers are concerned that a child is exhibiting symptoms of ADHD, they should see a pediatrician or ADHD specialist for a comprehensive evaluation and diagnosis.

Definition of ADHD

ADHD stands for attention-deficit/hyperactivity disorder. It is a neurobiological disorder that typically manifests itself in attention problems, hyperactivity and impulsivity. ADHD usually occurs in childhood, but can also be diagnosed in adults. The symptoms of ADHD can vary from person to person, but typical signs include difficulty concentrating or organizing tasks, impulsivity, restlessness, constant interruption of conversations or activities, forgetfulness or an increased risk-taking tendency. ADHD can affect academic performance, disrupt social behavior and increase the risk of mental health problems such as depression or anxiety. The treatment of ADHD usually involves a combination of behavioral and medication therapy as well as support through psychological counseling and training for those affected and their families. ADHD (attention deficit hyperactivity disorder) is a common neurodevelopmental disorder that can occur in children. The exact prevalence of ADHD in children depends on many factors, such as the definition criteria, research methods and sample selection. It is generally estimated that around 5 to 10 percent of children and adolescents worldwide are affected by ADHD. In some countries, the figures are higher or lower. In the USA, for example, around 11 percent of children aged 4 to 17 have been diagnosed with ADHD symptoms, while in Germany the estimated prevalence is 5 to 7 percent. It is important to note that ADHD is not a "one-size-fits-all" disorder, but that there are various subtypes that can differ in their symptoms and manifestations. The frequency of the different subtypes can therefore also vary.

Causes of ADHD

The causes of ADHD (attention deficit hyperactivity disorder) in children are complex and cannot be attributed to a single cause. However, there are a number of factors that can increase the risk of ADHD, including Genetics: ADHD has been found to run more frequently in families and certain genes may be linked to the disorder. Neurotransmitters: The disorder is associated with an imbalance of neurotransmitters (messengers in the brain) such as dopamine and noradrenaline, which are important for regulating attention, motivation and emotions. Brain structure and function: Studies have shown that in children with ADHD, certain areas of the brain that are important for regulating attention, impulse control and behavior control may be altered. Environmental factors: Early childhood stress, unhealthy diet and high exposure to environmental toxins can also increase the risk for ADHD. It is important to note that not all children exposed to one or more of these risk factors will develop ADHD. The disorder is the result of a complex interaction between genetics and environmental factors, and further research is needed to better understand the exact causes of ADHD.

Symptoms of ADHD in children

ADHD stands for attention-deficit/hyperactivity disorder and is a neurological disorder that is often diagnosed in children. Here are some symptoms of ADHD in children: Inattention: children with ADHD often have difficulty focusing their attention on a specific task and wandering off. They may have difficulty concentrating and often seem distracted. Hyperactivity: Children with ADHD can be overly fidgety and often do not behave calmly. They may have difficulty sitting still and may have a tendency to constantly get up or walk around. Impulsivity: Children with ADHD may have difficulty controlling their actions. They may act impulsively before thinking about the consequences of their actions. Listening problems: Children with ADHD may have difficulty following directions or instructions. They may forget what they have been told or become easily distracted. Difficulty organizing: Children with ADHD may have difficulty organizing their tasks and activities and may often lose their things. Forgetfulness: Children with ADHD may have difficulty remembering important information or appointments and can often forget important details. It is important to note that these symptoms can be within the normal range in children. ADHD should always be diagnosed by a qualified professional.

Restlessness and impulsivity

ADHD stands for Attention Deficit Hyperactivity Disorder and is a neurobiological developmental disorder that occurs in children and manifests itself through symptoms such as restlessness and impulsivity. These symptoms can interfere with children's daily lives and affect their academic and social skills. Children with ADHD may have difficulty sitting still, focusing their attention on tasks or activities, adhering to rules and controlling their impulses. They may also have difficulty organizing their thoughts and managing their time effectively. The restlessness and impulsivity in children with ADHD can show up in a variety of situations, such as at play, at school or at home. However, these symptoms can also vary from child to child and may differ from day to day. There are several treatment options for ADHD, including medication, therapy and behavioral interventions. Early diagnosis and treatment can help children with ADHD better control their symptoms and have more successful relationships and experiences in life.

Difficulty concentrating

Children with ADHD may have difficulty concentrating on tasks or activities that are boring or uninteresting. They may also be easily distracted and have difficulty focusing their attention on things that do not interest them. There are several strategies that parents and teachers can use to help children with ADHD improve their concentration. Here are some tips: Create a quiet environment: children with ADHD can be easily distracted by distractions such as loud noises, talking or movement. A quiet environment can help them focus better. Break tasks into smaller steps: Children with ADHD can feel overwhelmed when faced with large tasks. By breaking tasks into smaller steps, you can help them focus better and complete their tasks successfully. Set clear expectations: Children with ADHD may have difficulty recognizing their own priorities and tasks. By setting clear expectations and goals, parents and teachers can help them improve their concentration and complete their tasks more effectively. Use visual aids: Children with ADHD can benefit from visual aids such as tables, charts and graphs. These tools can help them better organize their tasks and improve their concentration. Use movement breaks: Children with ADHD often have difficulty sitting still for long periods of time. Incorporating movement breaks into the classroom or work routine can help them discharge their energy and focus better. It is important that children with ADHD are supervised by professionals who can help them manage their concentration difficulties. However, parents and teachers can also make a big contribution by offering them the strategies mentioned above.

Hyperactivity

Hyperactivity in children is a condition in which children exhibit excessive levels of physical activity and impulsivity. It is a symptom of attention-deficit/hyperactivity disorder (ADHD) and can also occur in other disorders such as anxiety, autism spectrum disorders and emotional disorders. Symptoms of hyperactivity in children may include: Constant movement that causes difficulty sitting or doing quiet activities Difficulty listening and following directions Impulsive behavior that can lead to mistakes or accidents Difficulty playing or working in groups Inattention and concentration problems If parents or guardians suspect that their child is suffering from hyperactivity, it is important that they consult a doctor or psychologist. Diagnosis of ADHD or other disorders requires a thorough clinical examination and may include various treatment options such as behavioral therapy, medication or a combination of both. Parents can also take certain steps to help their child, such as creating a structured environment that includes clear rules and routines that support the child's behavior and implementing reward systems to encourage positive behavior. It is also important to have open communication with the child's teacher to ensure that the child receives support at school as well.

Other possible symptoms

Here are some other possible symptoms that can occur in children with ADHD: Difficulty organizing tasks and activities Problems performing tasks and sustaining attention for long periods of time Delays or difficulty acquiring language and motor skills compared to other children Forgetfulness and loss of objects, Difficulty perceiving social cues and problems interacting with other children Impulsive or risky behavior that can lead to injury Difficulty falling asleep and waking up in the morning Sensitivity to stimuli such as noise or smells Mood swings and emotional outbursts, such as tantrums or tears Difficulty developing friendships and social relationships. It is important to note that ADHD can be different for each child and that not all children with ADHD will show all symptoms. If you suspect symptoms of

ADHD in your child, you should consult a pediatrician or child psychiatry specialist to get an accurate diagnosis and appropriate treatment.

Diagnosis of ADHD in children

The diagnosis of ADHD (attention-deficit/hyperactivity disorder) in children is usually made by a specialist or a child psychiatrist. Here are some steps that are commonly taken when diagnosing ADHD in children: Assessment of symptoms: The doctor will interview the patient and their parents or caregivers to get an understanding of what symptoms the child is exhibiting. Typical symptoms of ADHD include difficulty concentrating, hyperactivity and impulsivity. The doctor may also conduct an assessment of behavior in different situations, such as at school and at home. Developmental history assessment: The doctor will examine the child's developmental history to ensure that no other conditions or factors, such as autism, depression or anxiety disorders, could be causing the symptoms of ADHD. Assessment of physical symptoms: The doctor will perform a physical examination to ensure that there are no physical illnesses or injuries that could be causing the symptoms of ADHD. Assessment of behavior and attention tests: the doctor may administer specific behavior and attention tests to assess the child's attention span, working memory, and other cognitive abilities. Assessment of information from teachers and other caregivers: The doctor may also gather information from teachers and other caregivers to get a more complete picture of the child's behavior. The diagnosis of ADHD in children requires a careful assessment of the child's symptoms and developmental history, as well as a review of behavioral and attention tests. It is important that the diagnosis is made by a specialist or child psychiatrist to ensure an accurate assessment of the child's condition.

Examinations and tests for diagnosis

The diagnosis of ADHD in children is usually made by a child and adolescent psychiatrist, child and adolescent psychotherapist or a child and adolescent psychologist. There are no definitive tests or examinations that can ensure an ADHD diagnosis. Instead, an ADHD diagnosis is usually made on the basis of information from various sources, including Clinical interviews with the child and their parents or caregivers to assess symptoms and their impact on the child's daily life. Questionnaires and behavioral observations to assess the symptoms of ADHD and rule out the presence of other disorders such as anxiety disorders or depression. Assessment of any medical or psychological history of the child and their family. Review of the child's school and social environment to assess the impact of ADHD symptoms on the child's daily life. Evaluation of the child's developmental history and cognitive abilities. In some cases, a pediatrician may also perform a physical exam to rule out the presence of physical illnesses or problems, such as thyroid issues or hearing and vision problems, that could be contributing to the ADHD symptoms. It is important to note that an ADHD diagnosis is usually only made if the child shows symptoms of ADHD that go well beyond what would be expected in other children of a similar age. An ADHD diagnosis should always be considered in the context of the individual child and their environment.

Diagnostic criteria according to DSM-5

The DSM-5 (Diagnostic and Statistical Manual of Mental Disorders, Fifth Edition) defines the following diagnostic criteria for ADHD in children: A persistent or recurrent inability to perform tasks that are developmentally appropriate and meet age-appropriate expectations. A lack of attention to tasks or activities that are not interesting or stimulating. This may manifest as difficulty maintaining concentration, lack of attention to detail, frequently losing things or being easily distracted by external stimuli. A lack of impulse control that manifests itself in excessive talking, interrupting others, impatiently waiting for an opportunity, or making quick decisions without adequate thought. The presence of these symptoms for at least six months and in at least two settings (e.g. home and school). Clinically significant impairment in academic, social or occupational functioning. Symptoms that cannot be better explained by another psychiatric disorder. Symptoms cannot be attributed solely to chronological or developmental delay. It is important to note that these criteria should only be established by a specialist psychiatrist or an experienced child and adolescent psychiatrist. How parents and teachers can contribute to the diagnosis. The diagnosis of ADHD (attention-deficit/hyperactivity disorder) in children usually requires a comprehensive assessment by professionals such as pediatricians, psychologists and psychiatrists. However, parents and teachers can help facilitate the process of diagnosis by carefully observing and providing information. Here are some ways parents and teachers can help support a diagnosis of ADHD in children: Observing the child's behavior: Parents and teachers should closely observe the child's behavior and be alert for signs of ADHD such as concentration problems, impulsivity, and excessive physical activity. Documenting symptoms: Parents and teachers can also keep journals or notes about the child's behavior to document symptoms and patterns that may indicate ADHD. Sharing information: Parents should communicate with the child's teachers and share information about the child's behavior at school. Teachers can also provide observations and reports from school that can help establish a diagnosis. Conducting assessments: Parents and teachers may also participate in conducting assessments that are part of the diagnostic process, such as questionnaires or interviews. Obtaining medical information: Parents should ensure that they provide the child's doctor with any relevant medical information that may be important to the diagnosis of ADHD. It is important to note that a diagnosis of ADHD is usually made by a medical specialist. However, parents and teachers can help to facilitate the process of diagnosis by carefully observing and providing information.

Impact of ADHD on family life

ADHD (attention deficit hyperactivity disorder) can have a major impact on family life, especially if left untreated. Here are some possible effects that ADHD can have on family life: Difficulty organizing and planning tasks: People with ADHD can have difficulty getting organized and planning their tasks. This can cause them to have difficulty fulfilling their responsibilities around the home, resulting in disorganization and chaos. Impulsive behavior: People with ADHD may act impulsively without realizing the consequences. This can lead to conflict and unpredictability, which can disrupt family life. Difficulty maintaining relationships: People with ADHD may have difficulty maintaining long-term relationships. They may have problems paying attention to other people's needs and feelings, which can lead to conflict and misunderstandings. Behavioral problems: People with ADHD may exhibit agitated behavior that can be difficult for their family members to manage. This can lead to conflict and frustration, especially when it comes to rules and discipline. Emotional instability: People with ADHD can be emotionally unstable due to their impulsive nature and difficulties with emotion regulation. This can lead to frequent emotional outbursts that can be difficult for their family members to handle. Exhaustion and overwhelm: Caring for a family member with ADHD can be very stressful for the rest of the family. This can leave family members exhausted and overwhelmed and struggling to meet their own needs. It is important to note that not all people with ADHD show the same symptoms and that the impact on family life can vary. However, early diagnosis and treatment of ADHD can help to minimize the impact on family life.

Difficulties in everyday life

Children with ADHD (attention deficit hyperactivity disorder) can experience various difficulties in everyday life that affect their day-to-day life. Here are some possible challenges: Difficulty concentrating: Children with ADHD often have difficulty focusing their attention on a task or a teacher. They can be easily distracted and have difficulty maintaining their attention. Impulsivity: Children with ADHD can be impulsive and act without thinking about the consequences. They may have difficulty controlling themselves and often have difficulty refraining from acting on their own impulses. Hyperactivity: Children with ADHD can be difficult to keep calm and often have difficulty sitting still or concentrating.

They can be restless and fidgety and have difficulty controlling their energy. Social difficulties: Children with ADHD may have difficulty forming relationships with other children. They may have difficulty understanding their own emotions and those of others and can often be perceived as intrusive or inappropriate. Organization problems: Children with ADHD may have difficulty organizing their time and tasks. They may have difficulty completing their homework or organizing their personal belongings. Learning problems: Children with ADHD may have difficulty learning in school. They may have difficulty concentrating, retaining information and completing their homework. It is important to note that not all children with ADHD have the same difficulties, and the severity of symptoms may vary from child to child. Individualized treatment and support from professionals such as doctors, therapists and teachers can help overcome these challenges and improve the child's life.

Stress for the family

ADHD (attention-deficit/hyperactivity disorder) can be a major burden on families, especially if a child in the family is affected. The symptoms of ADHD can cause children to be impulsive, inattentive and hyperactive. These behaviors can have an impact on the family, as parents and siblings often have to cope with additional responsibilities and stress. A child with ADHD often needs extra care and attention from their parents in order to be successful. Parents may have difficulty controlling their child's behavior and setting consistent rules and limits. Children with ADHD may also have difficulty sticking to routines and tasks, such as homework or chores. This can result in parents having to invest extra time and energy to support their child. Siblings can also be affected by the situation, as they may receive less attention and time from their parents when a child with ADHD is in the house. They may also suffer from their sibling's behavior, especially if it is impulsive or aggressive. It is important that families of children with ADHD receive support to cope with the stress this disorder can place on their families. Parents can benefit from counseling and support groups to learn strategies to cope with their child's behavior. Family therapy can also help bring family members together and improve communication and interaction within the family. There are also many resources and support for children with ADHD, such as school counseling and medical treatment.

Dealing with difficult situations

Children with ADHD can often exhibit challenging behavior in difficult situations, which can be difficult for parents and caregivers to manage. Here are some strategies that can help: Structure and routine: children with ADHD need a clear structure and routine to feel safe and stable. A clear routine can help reduce stress and anxiety and avoid unexpected situations. Positive reinforcement: Reinforce positive behavior by praising and rewarding it. This can help children improve their behavior. Clear instructions: Give clear and precise instructions and break down complex tasks into small, easy-to-understand steps. Breaks and relaxation: Breaks and relaxation are important to reduce stress. Plan breaks and activities to relax. Empathy and understanding: Show empathy and understanding for the difficulties the child with ADHD is facing. Talk about their feelings and make them feel understood. Consequences: Set clear consequences for inappropriate behavior and stick to them. Consequences should be fair, predictable and consistent. Support: Seek support from a professional, such as a therapist or counselor, to help you deal with difficult situations. It is important to note that every child with ADHD is different and has individual needs. Some strategies that work for one child may not work for another. It often takes patience, creativity and flexibility to find an appropriate strategy for each child.

Impact of ADHD on school

ADHD (Attention Deficit Hyperactivity Disorder) can affect children's academic performance and behavior in a number of ways. Effects of ADHD on school Difficulty concentrating: Children with ADHD often have difficulty concentrating, especially on boring or repetitive tasks. This can lead to difficulties in understanding learning content and completing homework. Hyperactivity and impulsivity: Children with ADHD may have difficulty sitting still and staying quiet. They may also make impulsive decisions without thinking about the consequences. This can lead to disruptions in class and social problems. Difficulty with organization: Children with ADHD may have difficulty organizing their tasks and sticking to schedules. This can lead to difficulties in completing tasks and projects. Problems with working memory and learning strategies: Children with ADHD may have difficulty storing and recalling information. They may also have difficulty developing effective learning strategies. Low self-esteem: Children with ADHD may develop low self-esteem due to their difficulties in school. They may feel frustrated, overwhelmed or misunderstood. It is important to note that not all children with ADHD have the same symptoms or difficulties. Some children may do well in school, while others may struggle. Individualized support and adjustments can alleviate symptoms and help children reach their full potential.

Difficulties in the classroom

ADHD (attention-deficit/hyperactivity disorder) can cause children to struggle in the classroom, as they may have difficulty sustaining attention and concentration and may exhibit impulsive behavior. Here are some possible difficulties ADHD children may have in the classroom: Attention span: children with ADHD may have difficulty focusing and maintaining their attention on a particular task or lesson. They may be easily distracted and struggle to concentrate. Impulsivity: ADHD children may have difficulty controlling their impulses, which can lead to impulsive behavior such as sudden outbursts or interruptions in class. Hyperactivity: Some ADHD children are very energetic and restless, which can make it difficult for them to sit still or concentrate. Organizational skills: Children with ADHD may have difficulty organizing and planning their tasks and homework, which can lead to frustration and incomplete assignments. Working memory: Children with ADHD may have difficulty retaining information in their working memory, making it difficult for them to follow instructions or retain information for tests. Teachers can use various strategies to support ADHD children in the classroom, such as visual aids and instructions, a clear and structured classroom environment, clear communication and feedback, and attention to breaks and movement activities. Working closely with parents can also be helpful to optimize support for the child at school and at home.

Dealing with teachers and classmates

Children with ADHD (attention deficit hyperactivity disorder) can have difficulty coping well at school, especially when dealing with teachers and classmates. Here are some tips that can help: Open communication: parents should talk openly with teachers about their child's ADHD. They can provide information about how the symptoms affect the child's behavior and how teachers can help. Clear rules: Teachers can set clear rules and expectations for behavior in the classroom. This provides structure and direction for the child with ADHD. Positive reinforcement: Praise the child for good performance and behavior. This can boost the child's self-confidence and help them feel better about themselves. Time management: Children with ADHD often have difficulty managing their time well. Teachers can help them with this by giving them schedules and to-do lists. Attention span: Children with ADHD may have difficulty focusing on a task for long periods of time. Teachers can help them by giving them regular breaks and allowing them to move around when they get restless. Social skills: Children with ADHD may also have difficulty getting along with their classmates. Teachers can help them develop social skills by teaching them how to communicate effectively and resolve conflicts. Working with parents: Teachers should work closely with parents to ensure that the child with ADHD receives support both at home and at school. It is important to note that each student with ADHD is different and therefore may have different needs. However, by working together, teachers and parents can create a positive and supportive environment that will help the child succeed.

Ways to provide support and encouragement

However, there are several ways that schools can help ADHD children to provide them with the best educational experience possible. Here are some of the ways ADHD children can be supported and encouraged at school: Individualized support: Schools can provide individualized support to ensure that each child's needs are met. This can be provided by a teacher or a special education professional. Behavior plans: Behavior plans can help manage ADHD children's behavior at school. These plans can help improve concentration and focus and control behavior in the classroom. Curriculum adaptation: Teachers can customize the curriculum to help ADHD children learn better. This can be done through the use of visual aids or by structuring lessons to include breaks and activities that promote focus and attention. Support from specialists: Schools can also offer support from specialists such as psychologists, occupational therapists or speech therapists to provide targeted help for ADHD children. Promotion of exercise and sport: Exercise and sport can help to improve the concentration and attention of ADHD children. Schools can therefore integrate exercise and sport into lessons to help pupils concentrate better. Positive reinforcement: Schools can use positive reinforcement to encourage ADHD children's behavior. This can be done through praise, rewards and recognition for good work. Parent and teacher training: Schools can also provide training for parents and teachers to help them manage and support ADHD children. It is important to note that not all ADHD children need the same support. Schools should look at each child's needs individually and provide tailored support to ensure that each child can learn successfully.

Impact of ADHD on leisure activities

ADHD (attention-deficit/hyperactivity disorder) can affect the recreational activities of affected children in a number of ways. Here are some possible effects of ADHD on leisure activities in children: Difficulty organizing and planning: Children with ADHD may have difficulty organizing and planning their leisure activities. They may have difficulty deciding on an activity or using their time effectively. Hyperactivity: Some children with ADHD have high levels of energy and may find it difficult to enjoy quiet leisure activities such as reading or coloring. They often prefer activities that require physical movement. Impulsivity: Children with ADHD may be more impulsive than other children and may be quick to engage in risky leisure activities. They may have difficulty adhering to rules and boundaries. Social difficulties: Children with ADHD may have difficulty making and maintaining friendships. This can affect their leisure activities, as many activities often take place in groups. Concentration difficulties: Children with ADHD may have difficulty focusing their attention on a particular activity. This can cause them to quickly lose interest in an activity and become bored quickly. To improve recreational activities for children with ADHD, parents and caregivers can use certain strategies, such as a clear routine and structure, clear instructions and expectations, and activities that are tailored to the child's interests and strengths. It may also be helpful to break activities into shorter segments and schedule breaks to maintain focus and avoid overstimulation.

Difficulties playing games and sports

Children with ADHD (attention deficit hyperactivity disorder) may have difficulty concentrating on and performing games and sports activities. Here are some possible reasons for this: Attention deficits: Children with ADHD may have difficulty focusing on one thing and maintaining their attention. In games and sports activities, this can mean that they are easily distracted and have difficulty following the rules or instructions. Hyperactivity: Children with ADHD can be hyperactive, which means they have excessive energy and have difficulty sitting or standing still. This can affect games and sports activities by making them restless, running around or distracted. Impulsivity: Children with ADHD can be impulsive, which means they have difficulty controlling or planning their actions. In games and sports activities, this can mean that they make unexpected decisions or react inappropriately. Social difficulties: Children with ADHD may have difficulty understanding or regulating social interactions. In games and sports activities, this may mean that they have difficulty cooperating with other children or sticking to the rules. Low self-esteem: Children with ADHD may have low self-esteem due to their difficulties in games and sports activities. They may feel that they are not good enough or that they are rejected by other children. It is important that parents, teachers and caregivers help children with ADHD to overcome their difficulties in games and sports activities. Strategies such as clear guidance and structure, positive reinforcement, peer support and targeted exercises to improve attention and self-regulation can help.

Dealing with friends and peers

Here are some tips that parents and caregivers can use to help children with ADHD Allow your child to have regular social interactions with peers to improve their skills in interacting with others. For example, play regularly with other children, organize group activities or arrange play dates. Practice social skills such as sharing, listening and conversation with your child. Play role-playing games to simulate different social scenarios and help your child develop appropriate behaviors. Create a supportive environment by addressing your child's needs for structure and routine. Make sure your child gets enough sleep and has a healthy diet to minimize irritability and mood swings. Encourage positive relationships by positively reinforcing your child's behavior. Praise your child when they interact successfully with others or make good choices to boost their self-confidence and self-esteem. Set clear boundaries and consequences to avoid inappropriate behavior. Explain to your child the impact of their behavior on others and help them develop alternative ways of acting. Encourage your child to pursue their interests and strengths and make friends with other children who have similar interests. This can help to boost your child's self-confidence and self-esteem. Work closely with your child's teachers and caregivers to ensure he is supported in school and other social settings. Ask for feedback and look for joint solutions to improve your child's social skills.

Encourage hobbies and interests

Children with ADHD often have difficulty focusing their attention on one thing and concentrating on one activity for long periods of time. This can make it difficult to find and maintain hobbies and interests. Here are some tips that can help parents and caregivers of children with ADHD to make it easier to encourage hobbies and interests: Allow a variety of activities: Children with ADHD often have a wide range of interests. Give them the opportunity to try different hobbies and activities to discover their strengths and interests. Make activities structured and predictable: Children with ADHD benefit from structure and predictability. Try to do activities at regular intervals to create a routine that helps the child stay focused. Offer rewards: Positive reinforcement can be especially effective for children with ADHD. Offer rewards for achieving goals or completing activities. Consider the child's interests: Children with ADHD often have specific interests and strengths. Take these into account when choosing activities and hobbies to stimulate and encourage the child's interest. Avoid overstimulation: Children with ADHD can easily feel overstimulated. Avoid activities or environments that are too loud or too hectic to help the child focus better. Work with a therapist or coach: A therapist or coach can recommend specific strategies to improve attention and concentration in children with ADHD and help them develop hobbies and interests.

Medication treatment for ADHD

Medication treatment for ADHD (attention deficit hyperactivity disorder) usually involves the use of stimulants or non-stimulant medications. The choice of medication depends on the individual situation and should always be made in consultation with a specialist. Stimulants such as methylphenidate and amphetamine derivatives are the most commonly used medications in the treatment of ADHD. These drugs increase the concentration of neurotransmitters in the brain, particularly dopamine and noradrenaline, which are important for regulating attention and behavior. The dosage is adjusted individually and can be increased or decreased as needed. Non-stimulant medications such as atomoxetine can also be used to treat ADHD. These medications affect the neurotransmitter norepinephrine in a different way than stimulants and may be an alternative for some patients. It is important to note that medication alone is not sufficient to treat ADHD. A combination of medication and non-medication therapy, including behavioral interventions and coaching, may provide the best results. In addition, the effects of medication should be carefully monitored to ensure that it is effective and does not cause negative side effects.

How medication works

ADHD medications mainly act on the central nervous system and can improve the symptoms of ADHD. There are two main types of ADHD medications: stimulants and non-stimulant medications. Stimulants such as methylphenidate (e.g. Ritalin) and amphetamine (e.g. Adderall) increase the activity of certain neurotransmitters such as dopamine and noradrenaline in the brain. These neurotransmitters are important for regulating attention, concentration and impulse control. By increasing neurotransmitter activity, stimulants can help reduce ADHD symptoms and improve behavior and performance. Non-stimulant medications such as atomoxetine (e.g. Strattera) work differently to stimulants by blocking the reuptake of noradrenaline in the brain. This increases the availability of noradrenaline in the brain, which in turn can help to reduce ADHD symptoms. It is important to note that the mode of action of ADHD medications is not fully understood and that individual response to medication may vary. It is important to take the medication under the supervision of a qualified doctor and to have regular check-ups to ensure that it is safe and effective. Different medications and their advantages and disadvantages There are various medications that can be used to treat ADHD. The advantages and disadvantages of these medications depend on various factors, such as the age of the patient, the severity of symptoms and individual reactions to the medication. Here are some of the most common medications and their pros and cons: Methylphenidate (e.g. Ritalin): Advantages: It is one of the most commonly prescribed medications for the treatment of ADHD. It can help reduce symptoms of hyperactivity and impulsivity and improve concentration. Disadvantages: It can cause some side effects such as headaches, nausea and sleep disturbances. It can also lead to a loss of appetite. Amphetamine (e.g. Adderall): Benefits: It can be very effective in treating ADHD symptoms, especially in adults. It can also help improve mood and boost self-esteem. Disadvantages: It can cause some side effects such as loss of appetite, sleep disturbances, nausea and nervousness. It can also lead to dependence, especially if not prescribed and monitored properly. Atomoxetine (e.g. Strattera): Benefits: It is a non-stimulant medication that is suitable for people with ADHD who cannot or do not want to take stimulants. It can help improve concentration and impulse control. Disadvantages: It can cause some side effects such as nausea, dizziness and sleep disturbances. It can also take several weeks to take full effect. Guanfacine (e.g. Intuniv): Benefits: It is a medication specifically designed to treat ADHD in children. It can help reduce hyperactivity and impulsivity and improve concentration. Disadvantages: It can cause some side effects such as dizziness, fatigue and abdominal pain. It can also take a few weeks to take full effect. It is important to note that each medication has different advantages and disadvantages and not every medication is suitable for every patient. Choosing the right medication should be done in consultation with a qualified doctor who will take into account the patient's individual needs and reactions.

Dealing with possible side effects

ADHD medications can have various side effects that can vary from person to person. Some possible side effects include: Loss of appetite or weight loss Sleep disturbances or fatigue Headache or dizziness Nausea or gastrointestinal problems Mood swings or irritability High blood pressure or heart arrhythmia It is important that you talk to your doctor about possible side effects before you start taking ADHD medication. Your doctor can help you assess possible side effects and may adjust the dosage or prescribe a different medication to minimize unwanted side effects. If you notice any side effects while taking ADHD medication, you should tell your doctor. Depending on the severity and nature of the side effects, your doctor may make a dosage adjustment or recommend alternative treatment options. It is also important that you do not stop taking ADHD medication or change the dosage on your own without consulting your doctor. This can lead to a relapse of ADHD symptoms or increase the risk of side effects.

Non-medication treatment of ADHD

ADHD (attention-deficit/hyperactivity disorder) cannot be treated with medication alone. There are also several non-medication approaches that can help treat ADHD. Some of these approaches include: Behavioral and cognitive therapy: this type of therapy focuses on changing certain behaviors and thought patterns associated with ADHD. It can help reduce problems such as impulsivity, inattention and hyperactivity. Diet: A healthy diet rich in nutrients such as omega-3 fatty acids, vitamins and minerals can help reduce ADHD symptoms. A diet rich in sugar and artificial colors can make symptoms worse. Exercise: Regular exercise and physical activity can help reduce ADHD symptoms by reducing energy and relieving stress. Sports such as yoga and tai chi can also help improve concentration and balance. Organization and structure: People with ADHD often benefit from an organized environment and a structured agenda. It can be helpful to create a daily to-do list to focus on important tasks and plan the day. Support from family and friends: Strong social support can help reduce ADHD symptoms by providing emotional support and practical help. Relaxation techniques: Techniques such as mindfulness meditation, yoga and progressive muscle relaxation can help reduce stress and anxiety and improve focus and attention. It is important to note that not all non-medication treatments are effective for everyone with ADHD. Each person with ADHD has different symptoms and needs, so it may be necessary to try different approaches to find what works best for them. It is also important to work with a qualified professional such as a psychiatrist or psychologist to determine the best treatment options for your specific situation.

Behavioral therapy

Behavioral therapy is an important non-medication treatment option for ADHD. It is based on the idea that people's behavior is shaped by their environment and experiences and that behavior change can be achieved through targeted interventions. Behavioral therapy for ADHD includes various approaches and techniques aimed at encouraging specific behaviors and reducing unwanted behavior patterns. Here are some examples of techniques used in behavioral therapy for ADHD: Task and time management: ADHD patients often have difficulty with organizing their daily lives, including managing tasks and sticking to schedules. An important technique is to develop specific strategies to overcome these challenges, such as using to-do lists or breaking tasks into smaller, more manageable chunks. Self-control: Behavior modification often requires improved self-control. ADHD patients can learn to monitor and control their impulses and actions by using certain behavioral rules and strategies, such as pausing before responding to allow time to think. Social skills: ADHD patients often have difficulty interacting with other people. Improving social skills, such as listening, expressing needs or showing empathy, can help improve relationships with family, friends and colleagues. Relaxation and stress management: Many ADHD patients experience stress and anxiety, which can lead to further behavioral problems. Relaxation and stress management techniques such as breathing exercises, yoga or meditation can help to reduce physical and emotional reactivity and promote better self-regulation. Behavioral therapy can be carried out individually or in groups and is often offered by specially trained therapists. The duration of therapy depends on individual needs and goals and can last from a few weeks to several months. In many cases, behavioral therapy is used in combination with medication to ensure comprehensive treatment.

Parent training

ADHD (attention deficit hyperactivity disorder) is a neurobiological disorder that can occur in children and adults. One non-medication-based treatment option for ADHD in children is parent training. Parent training is a structured program that aims to improve parents' ability to support and educate their child with ADHD. The program is based on the idea that parents can learn to parent their child in a way that reduces their symptoms of ADHD and promotes their strengths. Parent training typically includes the following steps: Psychoeducation: Parents are taught about ADHD and how it affects their child's behavior. Behavior management: Parents learn how to improve their child's behavior through positive reinforcement and consequences. Problem solving: Parents learn how to address problems and conflicts with their child. Communication: Parents learn how to communicate more effectively with their child and improve their relationship. Self-care: Parents learn how to help themselves to reduce their own stress levels and exhaustion. Parent training can be delivered in group or individual sessions. It can also be led by a therapist or a specialized coach. The duration of the program varies, but it is usually conducted over a period of several weeks or months. Parent training has been shown to be very effective in improving the behavior of children with ADHD. It can also improve the relationship between parents and children and help parents to take better care of themselves. Parent training is a non-drug treatment option for ADHD that is often used in combination with other treatment methods, such as behavioral or occupational therapy.

Occupational therapy

Occupational therapy can be a useful non-drug treatment option for ADHD. Occupational therapists work with people of all ages to help them manage their daily activities and improve their independence. They can also help people with ADHD to alleviate their symptoms and improve their behavior. Below are some ways that occupational therapy can be used in the treatment of ADHD: Structuring daily routines: occupational therapists can help people with ADHD structure their daily routines by teaching them how to use their time more effectively and prioritize. Improving fine motor skills: Occupational therapists can also work on improving fine motor skills to improve writing and reading skills. Improving social skills: Occupational therapists can also work with people with ADHD on improving their social skills to help them communicate better with others and exhibit socially acceptable behavior. Relaxation techniques: Occupational therapists can also use relaxation techniques such as yoga or breathing exercises to help people with ADHD improve their anxiety and impulse control. Improving organizational skills: People with ADHD often have difficulty organizing and planning their tasks. Occupational therapists can help them improve their organizational skills to help them complete their tasks more effectively. Overall, occupational therapy can be a valuable tool to help people with ADHD alleviate their symptoms and improve their quality of life. However, it is important to note that occupational therapy alone is not a complete treatment for ADHD and that a combination of medication and non-medication treatment methods is often most effective.

Other options for therapy and support

ADHD (attention deficit hyperactivity disorder) can also be treated and supported by non-drug treatment options. Here are some examples: Behavioral therapy: this type of therapy can help improve certain behaviors and habits in people with ADHD. There are different types of behavioral therapy, such as cognitive behavioral therapy or behavior modification, that are tailored to the patient's individual needs and difficulties. Parent training: Parents can be specially trained to help their children with ADHD. Parents learn strategies and techniques to improve their child's behavior, enhance their skills and help them interact better with other people. Occupational therapy: This therapy aims to improve the patient's daily living skills to help them cope better at school, work or home. This includes, for example, time management, organization, self-regulation and fine motor skills. Sport and exercise: Sport and exercise can help to improve the concentration and cognitive skills of people with ADHD. It can also help to reduce stress and anxiety. Diet and supplements: Although there is no specific diet that can cure ADHD, a balanced diet can help reduce symptoms. Some supplements such as omega-3 fatty acids or zinc can also help improve symptoms. Sleep hygiene: Adequate and regular sleep is important for the health and well-being of people with ADHD. It is important to practice good sleep hygiene, such as having regular bedtimes and avoiding stimulants such as caffeine. It is important to note that non-medication therapies and support for ADHD should be individualized to the patient. A combination of therapies and support options can often be most effective. It is important to consult a qualified doctor or therapist to find the right treatment option.

Diet and ADHD

There is some evidence that diet can have an impact on the symptoms of ADHD (attention-deficit/hyperactivity disorder). A healthy diet with balanced meals, plenty of fruit and vegetables and sufficient water can help to improve the symptoms of ADHD. One possible explanation for this is that certain nutrients and vitamins included in a healthy diet can improve brain function. For example, omega-3 fatty acids found in fish, flaxseed and walnuts are known to support cognitive function. One study found that omega-3 fatty acids can help improve attention and behavior in children with ADHD. There is also evidence that certain foods can exacerbate the symptoms of ADHD. Some studies have shown that sugar and foods with a high glycemic index (GI) can exacerbate the symptoms of ADHD. The GI is a measure of how quickly a food raises blood sugar levels. Foods with a high GI can raise blood sugar levels quickly and then drop quickly, which can lead to mood swings and lack of energy. It is important to note that the effects of diet on ADHD can vary from person to person. There is no specific dietary recommendation for ADHD that is suitable for all sufferers. If you or your child has ADHD, you should speak with a doctor or nutritionist to develop the best dietary strategy.

The link between diet and ADHD

There is some evidence that diet may have a link to ADHD (attention deficit hyperactivity disorder). However, there is no clear evidence of a causal relationship between diet and the development of ADHD. Some studies have shown that certain food additives and preservatives, such as artificial colors, preservatives and flavor enhancers, can increase symptoms in some children with ADHD. There is also evidence that an inadequate supply of certain nutrients such as omega-3 fatty acids, iron, zinc, magnesium and vitamin B6 can exacerbate symptoms in some children with ADHD. In addition, there is evidence that a healthy diet rich in fruits, vegetables, whole grains, lean protein and healthy fats can help treat ADHD by helping to keep blood sugar levels stable and balancing brain chemistry. However, it is important to note that diet is only one part of a comprehensive treatment approach for ADHD. Other treatment options include behavior modification, medication and psychotherapy. It is also important that parents of children with ADHD work with a qualified healthcare provider to develop an individualized treatment strategy.

Recommendations for an adequate diet

A balanced diet can help alleviate the symptoms of ADHD. Here are some recommendations for an adequate diet for ADHD: Eat a balanced diet: Make sure you eat a balanced diet with a variety of foods, including fruits, vegetables, whole grains, lean protein and healthy fats. Avoid sugary and processed foods: These can cause a spike in blood sugar levels and lead to an increase in hyperactivity and impulsivity. Eat regularly: Eat small meals regularly to keep your blood sugar levels stable and avoid cravings. Avoid foods that can cause allergic reactions: Certain foods, such as dairy, wheat and soy, can cause allergic reactions in some people and contribute to ADHD symptoms. Consume omega-3 fatty acids: Omega-3 fatty acids, found in fatty fish such as salmon, tuna and herring, as well as nuts and seeds, can help improve brain function and alleviate ADHD symptoms. Drink enough water: Make sure you drink enough water to stay hydrated and ensure optimal brain function. Consider supplementation: Supplements such as vitamin B6, zinc and magnesium can help alleviate ADHD symptoms. However, it is important to discuss this with a doctor or nutritionist before taking any supplements. It is also important to note that adequate nutrition alone may not be enough to fully treat ADHD symptoms. A combination of a balanced diet, regular physical activity and, if necessary, medication or behavioral therapy can be helpful in treating ADHD.

Avoiding certain foods

There is some research that suggests that certain foods or food groups can affect the symptoms of ADHD (attention deficit hyperactivity disorder). However, these findings are not conclusive and there are no clear recommendations on diet for ADHD yet. Some studies have shown that certain foods such as sugar, artificial colors and preservatives can exacerbate the symptoms of ADHD in some children. However, other studies have shown no significant effect on the symptoms of ADHD. There is also some evidence that a balanced diet with sufficient omega-3 fatty acids, vitamins and minerals can have a positive impact on the symptoms of ADHD. A balanced diet can also help to improve overall health and well-being, which can have a positive impact on ADHD symptoms. It is important that everyone looks at their diet individually and pays attention to how certain foods affect their symptoms. Some people with ADHD may find that they should avoid certain foods or food groups, while others may not notice any effects. It's also important to consult with a doctor or nutritionist to make sure you're getting all the necessary nutrients needed for optimal health.

Sport and exercise for ADHD

Sports and exercise can be very helpful for ADHD (attention deficit hyperactivity disorder) as they can positively affect concentration, mood and behavior. Here are some ways in which sport and exercise can help with ADHD: Improve concentration: regular physical activity can help improve concentration in people with ADHD. Exercise provides oxygen and nutrients to the brain, which can boost brain function and attention. Reducing impulsivity and hyperactivity: Sport and exercise can help to calm the overactive part of the brain and improve impulse control. This can help reduce impulsive behavior and hyperactivity. Reducing stress and anxiety: Sport and exercise can help to reduce stress and anxiety. Physical activity releases endorphins, which act as natural painkillers and can create a sense of relaxation and well-being. Improving self-confidence: Regular exercise can help to improve self-confidence and self-perception in people with ADHD. Through success in sport, sufferers can develop a sense of achievement and self-worth. Improving social skills: Sports and exercise can also help improve social skills. By participating in team sports or group activities, people with ADHD can learn to interact with others and develop conflict resolution skills. It is important to note that each person with ADHD has different needs and abilities. Therefore, it is important that the type and intensity of physical activity is individualized. A combination of aerobic exercise, such as running, cycling and swimming, as well as activities that promote coordination and balance, such as yoga or tai chi, can be a good choice. It is also important that sport and exercise are fun in order to maintain motivation.

Effect of sport and exercise on ADHD symptoms

There is scientific evidence that sport and exercise can have a positive effect on the symptoms of ADHD (attention deficit hyperactivity disorder). Some of the positive effects may include: Improvement in cognitive function: Exercise and sport can help to improve attention, working memory and overall cognitive function. This can be particularly beneficial for people with ADHD, who often have difficulty controlling their attention. Reducing stress and anxiety: Exercise and sport can help to reduce stress and anxiety, which can often accompany ADHD. Exercise can also help to improve mood and boost self-esteem. Improving physical health: Sport and exercise can help to control weight, lower blood pressure and reduce the risk of heart disease and other health problems. This can be particularly beneficial for people with ADHD, which is more commonly associated with being overweight or obese than other mental health conditions. Improving sleep quality: Regular physical activity can help improve sleep quality. A good night's sleep is particularly important for people with ADHD, as a lack of sleep can exacerbate symptoms. However, it is important to note that sport and exercise are not a cure for ADHD and cannot alleviate all symptoms. It can be a complementary therapy option, but medication or other therapies such as behavioral therapy may also be necessary. It is also important to consider individual needs and abilities and create an appropriate exercise plan to avoid injury or overexertion.

Suitable sports for children with ADHD

There are many suitable sports for children with ADHD that can help them burn off excess energy, improve their ability to concentrate and strengthen their social skills. Here are some options: Team sports such as soccer, basketball, baseball or field hockey can help improve social skills and teach children to work as a team. Martial arts such as karate or judo are often popular with children with ADHD as they require self-control and concentration. Swimming is a great way to improve coordination and breathing and can also help relieve stress. Dance or gymnastics classes can help improve motor skills and coordination, as well as boost self-confidence and creativity. Cycling or running outdoors is also a good option as it can help children relax and enjoy the outdoors. It is important to find a sport that the child enjoys and likes to do to keep motivation high. It is also important that the activity is regular and structured to help children improve their concentration and discipline. Integrating exercise into everyday life People with ADHD can often have difficulty concentrating on a task or staying calm. However, exercise can help alleviate the symptoms of ADHD and improve concentration. Here are some tips on how to incorporate exercise into everyday life: Take movement breaks: taking a short break to move and stretch can help increase blood flow and stimulate the brain. These breaks can also be used to perform a short exercise routine, e.g. a few push-ups or squats. Choose activities that are fun: Choosing activities that are fun can increase motivation to exercise. Activities such as dancing, skateboarding or trampolining can be particularly appealing.

Integrate sport into everyday life

Sports such as jogging, cycling or swimming can also be integrated into everyday life. For example, you can cycle to work or school or go for a walk during your lunch break. Use exercise as a reward: Exercise can also be used as a reward. For example, after completing a task, you can allow yourself to go for a run around the block or do a short yoga session. Exercise together: Exercising with friends or family can not only be more fun, but can also increase motivation. Going for a walk or a bike ride with friends can be a great way to exercise and socialize. It is important to realize that everyone has different needs and preferences. It is therefore advisable to try out different types of exercise and find out what works best for you. Sleep and ADHD There are studies that show a link between sleep problems and attention deficit hyperactivity disorder (ADHD) in children and adults. People with ADHD often have difficulty falling asleep or staying asleep, which can lead to sleep disorders. On the other hand, lack of sleep can also exacerbate the symptoms of ADHD. It is believed that sleep disorders in ADHD patients may be due to a dysfunction in the area of the brain responsible for regulating sleep-wake cycles. Treating sleep disorders can therefore also help to reduce ADHD symptoms. Therapy to improve sleep may include regulating the sleep-wake cycle, learning relaxation techniques or taking medication. However, it is important that the treatment is individually tailored to the patient's needs. Medication should only be prescribed and monitored by a doctor.

Sleep disorders in children with ADHD

It is known that children with ADHD suffer from sleep problems more often than children without ADHD. There are various reasons for sleep disorders in children with ADHD, such as Hyperactivity: children with ADHD may have difficulty calming down and settling down, which can lead to sleep disturbances. Impulsivity: Children with ADHD may have difficulty controlling their impulses, which can cause them to go to bed late and have difficulty falling asleep. Medication: The medications used to treat

ADHD can affect sleep. Some medications can cause children to have difficulty falling asleep, while others can promote sleep. Anxiety and depression: Children with ADHD have a higher risk of also suffering from anxiety or depression. These can also lead to sleep problems. There are several steps parents and caregivers can take to reduce sleep disturbances in children with ADHD, such as: Establishing a sleep routine: A regular bedtime and evening ritual can help children sleep better. Creating a quiet sleep environment: A quiet and dark sleep environment can help children fall asleep faster and sleep better. Limiting screen time: Limiting the amount of time children spend in front of a screen before bedtime can help them fall asleep faster and sleep better. Physical activity: Regular physical activity can help children calm down and exhaust themselves, which can lead to better sleep. Discuss sleep problems with a doctor: If sleep problems are severe in children with ADHD, it may be helpful to talk to a doctor about possible treatment options.

Causes of sleep problems

Children with ADHD often have difficulty falling asleep and staying asleep. The exact causes of sleep problems in children with ADHD are not fully understood, but there are some factors that may play a role: Overactive mind: children with ADHD often have an overactive mind and may have difficulty calming down and settling down. This can cause them to have difficulty falling asleep. Impulsivity: Children with ADHD can be impulsive and tend to act impulsively without thinking about it. This can cause them to have difficulty sticking to a regular bedtime. Medication: Medications used to treat ADHD can interfere with sleep. Some stimulants can disrupt the sleep-wake cycle and cause insomnia. Sleep apnea: Children with ADHD have a higher risk of sleep apnea, a condition in which breathing is interrupted during sleep. This can lead to sleep disturbances and other health problems. Anxiety: Children with ADHD may also have anxieties that keep them awake. For example, they may worry that they won't do well in school or that they won't be able to complete their assignments. Environmental factors: There are also some environmental factors that can affect the sleep of children with ADHD, such as noise, light and restlessness in the environment. It is important that parents and caregivers of children with ADHD talk to a doctor to identify the causes of sleep problems and take appropriate measures to improve sleep. Measures to improve sleep Children with ADHD (attention deficit hyperactivity disorder) can often struggle to sleep well. Here are some measures that can help improve sleep in children with ADHD: Regular daily routine: a regular daily routine helps the body to adjust to specific times for sleeping and waking. Try to get the child to bed and up at the same time every day, even on weekends. Create a calming sleeping environment: Darken the room and keep it cool. Make sure the bed is comfortable and that the child has comfortable bedding. Restrictions on caffeine: Caffeine can disrupt sleep. Try to avoid consuming caffeinated drinks such as cola, tea or coffee in the afternoon and evening. Avoid excitement just before bedtime: Avoid activities that excite or stimulate the child just before bedtime. This includes computer games, television or exciting books. Regular physical activity: Regular physical activity can help children with ADHD to relax and sleep better. Try to plan an activity every day that challenges the child physically. Relaxation techniques: Relaxation techniques such as progressive muscle relaxation or yoga can help calm the child before bedtime. Medication: In some cases, medication can help improve sleep in children with ADHD. Talk to a health care professional about the options. It's important to note that everyone is different and what works for one child may not work for another. It may take some trial and error to figure out which sleep interventions work best for the child.

ADHD and comorbidities

ADHD (attention-deficit/hyperactivity disorder) is a neurological disorder characterized by a combination of symptoms that affect attention, impulse control and hyperactivity. It is known that ADHD is often associated with other psychiatric disorders, known as comorbidities. Some of the most common comorbidities in ADHD are: Autism spectrum disorders (ASD) Emotional regulation disorders (e.g., depression, anxiety disorders, bipolar disorder) Tic disorders (e.g., Tourette syndrome) Learning difficulties (e.g., reading and spelling disorders, dyscalculia) Substance abuse and dependence Sleep disorders Eating disorders It is important to note that the presence of comorbidities can complicate the diagnosis and treatment of ADHD. Careful diagnosis and a holistic approach are necessary to treat both ADHD and any co-occurring disorders. Individualized treatment planning should also take into account comorbidities and include specific therapy where appropriate to achieve the best possible results. Frequency of comorbidities ADHD (attention deficit hyperactivity disorder) is often associated with other psychiatric disorders or health problems, which is referred to as comorbidity. The prevalence of comorbidities in ADHD can vary by study and sample, but here are some common comorbidities in ADHD: Social behavior disorders: up to 40% of children and adolescents with ADHD Anxiety disorders: up to 30-40% of children and adolescents and up to 25-40% of adults with ADHD Mood disorders (depression, bipolar disorder): up to 20-30% of adults with ADHD Addictive disorders (alcohol, drugs): up to 20-30% of adults with ADHD Eating disorders (e.g. bulimia, binge eating disorder): up to 20-30% of adults with ADHD. Eating disorders (e.g. bulimia, binge eating disorder): up to 20% of adults with ADHD Sleep disorders: up to 50% of children and adolescents and up to 30-40% of adults with ADHD It is important to note that these figures may vary and that there may be other comorbidities that are not included in this list. It is also possible for a person with ADHD to have no comorbidities.

Relationship between ADHD and other mental disorders

ADHD (attention-deficit/hyperactivity disorder) is a neurological disorder characterized by problems with attention, impulse control and hyperactivity. There are some mental disorders that are commonly associated with ADHD: Anxiety disorders: People with ADHD have a higher risk of anxiety disorders such as Generalized Anxiety Disorder, Social Anxiety Disorder and Panic Disorder. Depression: Depression is a common side effect of ADHD. This is thought to be due to the difficulties in maintaining relationships and performing at school or work, as well as the chronic stress and overwhelm associated with ADHD. Obsessive-compulsive spectrum disorders (OCD): There is an increased likelihood that people with ADHD also suffer from obsessive-compulsive disorders such as compulsive actions or thoughts. Addiction: People with ADHD have an increased risk of substance abuse and addiction. Personality disorders: There is evidence that ADHD is associated with some personality disorders such as Borderline Personality Disorder, Antisocial Personality Disorder and Narcissistic Personality Disorder. It is important to note that not everyone with ADHD also has another mental disorder, but there is an increased likelihood that this is the case. Correct diagnosis and a comprehensive treatment approach are important to ensure the best possible care for people with ADHD and other mental disorders.

Diagnosis and treatment of comorbidities

ADHD (attention-deficit/hyperactivity disorder) is often associated with other conditions or disorders, known as comorbidities. The most common comorbidities in ADHD are anxiety disorders, depression, social behavior disorders, tic disorders and learning difficulties. Comprehensive diagnosis and treatment of comorbidities is important to improve the quality of life of affected individuals and minimize the long-term effects of the disorders. Diagnosis: The diagnosis of comorbidities in ADHD is made through a comprehensive clinical examination and history taking. It may also be necessary to perform specific tests and questionnaires to confirm or rule out comorbidity. Accurate diagnosis of comorbidities is important because the symptoms of ADHD and other disorders may be similar, which can lead to misdiagnosis and inappropriate treatment. The treatment of comorbidities in ADHD is often complex and often involves a combination of medication and therapy. Treating ADHD is often the first step in treating comorbidities, as controlling ADHD symptoms can help reduce or eliminate other symptoms. Medications such as stimulants can be effective in treating ADHD and some comorbidities such as depression and anxiety disorders.

Therapy can also be an important part of treating comorbidities. Various therapies such as cognitive behavioral therapy (CBT), family therapy, and psychoeducation can help reduce symptoms of comorbidities and improve quality of life. Treatment for learning difficulties such as dyslexia or dyscalculia may also be necessary to improve academic performance. It is important to emphasize that the treatment of comorbidities in ADHD should be individualized, as each case is unique. A comprehensive diagnosis and close collaboration between the patient, the treating physician and other therapists are important to ensure the best possible treatment.

Dealing with ADHD in nursery school

ADHD (attention-deficit/hyperactivity disorder) can be a challenge for children, parents and teachers at kindergarten age. Here are some tips for dealing with ADHD in kindergarten: Show understanding: It is important that preschool teachers have an understanding of the symptoms of ADHD in order to better understand the child's behavior and respond appropriately. Create structure and routine: Children with ADHD benefit from a structured and predictable environment. Teachers can, for example, introduce fixed rituals for the daily routine and establish clear rules. Give clear and brief instructions: Children with ADHD can have difficulty understanding and implementing complex instructions. It is important to give clear and brief instructions and to repeat or visualize them if necessary. Use positive reinforcement: Children with ADHD benefit from positive reinforcement for good behavior. Teachers can, for example, give praise when the child remains sitting quietly or has completed a task. Take exercise breaks: Children with ADHD often have a high need for exercise. It can be helpful to take movement breaks to help the child concentrate and release energy. Cooperation with parents: Close cooperation with parents is important in order to coordinate the child's behavior in kindergarten and at home and to develop joint strategies. Special requirements in kindergarten Children with ADHD (attention deficit hyperactivity disorder) often have special requirements in kindergarten, as they may have difficulty concentrating on a task, act impulsively and have high energy levels. Here are some requirements that should be considered in kindergarten for ADHD: Structure and routine: children with ADHD benefit from a structured daily routine that has clear rules and routines. A visual daily schedule can help give children an idea of what's coming next. Clear instructions: Children with ADHD may have difficulty focusing on a task, especially if it is not clearly explained. Therefore, instructions should be simple and clear. It can also be helpful to give instructions verbally and visually. Positive reinforcement: Children with ADHD often respond well to positive reinforcement. This means that they should be rewarded for good behavior instead of being punished for bad behavior. Small groups: Children with ADHD can benefit from smaller groups as they find it easier to focus and interact with others. Exercise: Children with ADHD often have high energy levels and therefore need regular opportunities to exercise. This can be encouraged, for example, through movement breaks or special exercises. Understanding staff: Kindergarten teachers should be informed about ADHD and have an understanding of the needs and behaviors of children with ADHD. Open communication with parents can help to ensure the best possible support for the child. It is important to emphasize that every child with ADHD is unique and has different needs. An individualized approach and collaboration between educators, parents and professionals can help ensure the best possible support for each child.

Promoting social skills

People with ADHD (attention-deficit/hyperactivity disorder) can have difficulty learning social skills and responding appropriately in social situations. Here are some strategies that can be used to promote social skills in ADHD: Social learning: a method that aims to improve social behavior by teaching skills such as conversational skills, empathy, and conflict resolution. There are several programs that specialize in social learning. Role-playing: A practical method of practicing social interactions by taking on different roles and acting out different situations. Role-playing can also be done in groups to improve understanding of social situations and empathy for others. Behavior modification: This method aims to change unwanted behavior through rewards and punishments. Positive reinforcement can be used to encourage good social behavior, while negative consequences can be used to discourage inappropriate behavior. Individual or group therapy: Cognitive behavioral therapy can help people with ADHD improve their social skills and learn to manage emotions and stress. Therapy can be carried out in individual or group formats.

Support for parents

When a kindergarten-aged child receives an ADHD diagnosis, it can be challenging for parents to cope and support their child appropriately. Here are some tips that can help: Educate yourself about ADHD: The more you know about ADHD, the better you can understand how the disorder affects your child and how you can help. Talk to your pediatrician, a therapist or an ADHD specialist to learn more about the symptoms, treatment options and strategies to help your child. Set clear rules and structure: Children with ADHD benefit from clear rules and structure to help them organize their tasks and behaviors. Create a schedule for your child's day and make sure they have regular meal times, rest times and play times. Provide targeted support: Children with ADHD may have difficulty concentrating, controlling their impulses and regulating their emotions. You can help them by offering specific support, such as giving brief instructions, breaking tasks into small steps, giving them a break or drawing their attention to positive behaviors. Work together with the kindergarten: Talk to the teachers and staff at the nursery about your child's needs. Together you can develop a strategy to help your child in the kindergarten routine. Encourage positive behavior: Praise your child for positive behaviors and accomplishments they achieve. Avoid focusing only on your child's difficulties, but also focus on their strengths and successes. Seek support: It can be helpful to join a support group for parents of children with ADHD or to seek therapy or counseling. Here you can exchange ideas with other parents and benefit from their experiences.

ADHD in elementary school

ADHD (attention-deficit/hyperactivity disorder) can manifest itself in children as early as elementary school. Some of the signs of ADHD in elementary school children may include: Difficulty sitting still and concentrating Impulsive behavior such as sudden interruptions or disruptive activities Problems organizing tasks and keeping schedules Difficulty following directions or following rules Difficulty establishing and maintaining friendships It is important to note that not all children who have difficulties in these areas necessarily have ADHD. There are many reasons why children may have difficulties in school. However, if these behaviors persist over a long period of time and interfere with the child's daily life, it is advisable to talk to a doctor or psychologist about the possibility of ADHD. Early diagnosis and treatment of ADHD can help children perform better in school and build more successful social relationships. Special challenges in elementary school Children with ADHD (attention-deficit/hyperactivity disorder) may face special challenges in elementary school. Here are some possible challenges that may arise: Difficulty concentrating: Children with ADHD may have difficulty concentrating for long periods of time, especially on tasks that do not seem interesting or challenging enough for them. This can affect their academic performance and lead to frustration. Impulsivity: Children with ADHD may have difficulty controlling impulses and avoiding inappropriate behavior. They may have difficulty sitting still or waiting their turn, and may have difficulty regulating their thoughts and feelings. Social interaction: Children with ADHD may have difficulty interacting appropriately in social situations. They may have difficulty listening, having conversations and making friends. They may also have difficulty understanding non-verbal cues such as body language and tone of voice. Organization and time management: Children with ADHD may have difficulty staying organized and using their time effectively. They may have difficulty completing homework, planning and organizing their assignments, and arriving on time for lessons and activities. Sensitivity to criticism: Children with ADHD may be particularly sensitive to criticism and may quickly feel discouraged. This can cause them to withdraw or give up their efforts if they feel they are not succeeding. It is important to note that each child with ADHD is unique and has different challenges. However, early identification and treatment of ADHD can help children succeed in school and reach their full potential.

Promoting concentration and motivation

ADHD (attention-deficit/hyperactivity disorder) can be challenging for children in elementary school, as it can be difficult to focus and stay motivated. However, there are some strategies and techniques that can help boost concentration and motivation for children with ADHD in elementary school. Here are some tips: Structure the day: children with ADHD benefit from a clear and structured daily routine. Schedule regular times for meals, homework and leisure activities. Reduce distractions: Reduce unnecessary distractions by clearing the classroom or child's work area of unnecessary items or by minimizing distracting noises. Use visual aids: Use pictures, colors and symbols to visualize important information and increase the child's attention. Use movement breaks: Integrate short movement breaks into the child's daily routine to give them the opportunity to burn off excess energy and improve their concentration. Give clear instructions: Make sure instructions are clear and relate to specific tasks. Provide positive reinforcement: Praise the child for good performance and progress to boost their self-esteem and increase their motivation. Work with parents: Work closely with parents to develop a shared understanding and consistent approach to supporting the child. It is also important to note that each child with ADHD has individual needs and may require a combination of different strategies and techniques to support the child's concentration and motivation. Collaboration between teachers, parents and, where appropriate, professionals such as a child psychologist or psychiatrist can be helpful in providing the best possible support for the child. Dealing with homework and exams can be particularly challenging for children with ADHD in elementary school. Here are some tips for parents and teachers to help them: Structure and organization: children with ADHD need a clear structure and routine. It is helpful to create a set schedule for homework and test preparation and discuss it with the child. A to-do list or a weekly schedule can also help to keep an overview. Positive reinforcement: Children with ADHD often have difficulty concentrating and completing their tasks. Praise and rewards for their efforts can help them stay motivated. It is also important to set realistic goals and recognize the child's progress. Take breaks: Children with ADHD often find it difficult to work for long periods of time. Breaks are important to give them time to relax and recover. It can be helpful to take short breaks after each completed task or longer breaks after a certain period of time. Reduce distractions: Children with ADHD can be easily distracted, especially by visual and auditory stimuli. It is helpful to minimize distractions such as television, cell phones or music during homework or study time. Teacher support: Teachers can provide support by giving clear instructions and expectations and providing regular feedback. It is also helpful to offer additional support in the form of tutoring or special learning programs. Collaboration between parents and teachers: Close collaboration between parents and teachers is important to monitor the child's progress and develop appropriate strategies to support them. It is important to note that every child with ADHD is different and has different needs. Individualized support and adaptation of strategies is therefore important.

Dealing with homework and exams

Dealing with homework and exams can be particularly challenging for children with ADHD in elementary school. Here are some tips for parents and teachers to help them: Structure and organization: children with ADHD need a clear structure and routine. It is helpful to create a set schedule for homework and test preparation and discuss it with the child. A to-do list or a weekly schedule can also help to keep an overview. Positive reinforcement: Children with ADHD often have difficulty concentrating and completing their tasks. Praise and rewards for their efforts can help them stay motivated. It is also important to set realistic goals and recognize the child's progress. Take breaks: Children with ADHD often find it difficult to work for long periods of time. Breaks are important to give them time to relax and recover. It can be helpful to take short breaks after each completed task or longer breaks after a certain period of time. Reduce distractions: Children with ADHD can be easily distracted, especially by visual and auditory stimuli. It is helpful to minimize distractions such as television, cell phones or music during homework or study time. Teacher support: Teachers can provide support by giving clear instructions and expectations and providing regular feedback. It is also helpful to offer additional support in the form of tutoring or special learning programs. Collaboration between parents and teachers: Close collaboration between parents and teachers is important to monitor the child's progress and develop appropriate strategies to support them. It is important to note that every child with ADHD is different and has different needs. Individualized care and adaptation of strategies is therefore important.

Imprint

Luna Ludwig
Am Anger 3
06869 Coswig
Germany
Luna-Publishing.de

www.ingramcontent.com/pod-product-compliance
Lightning Source LLC
Chambersburg PA
CBHW070748260726

48660CB00007B/3018